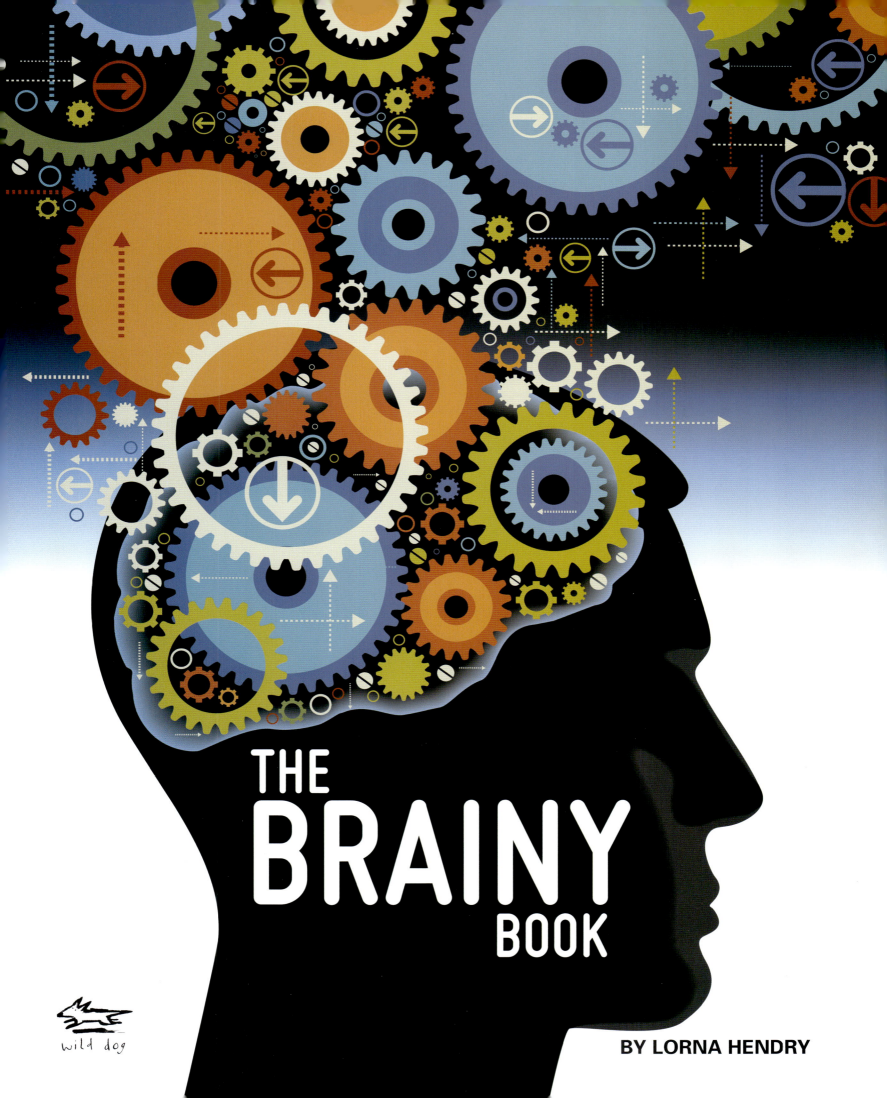

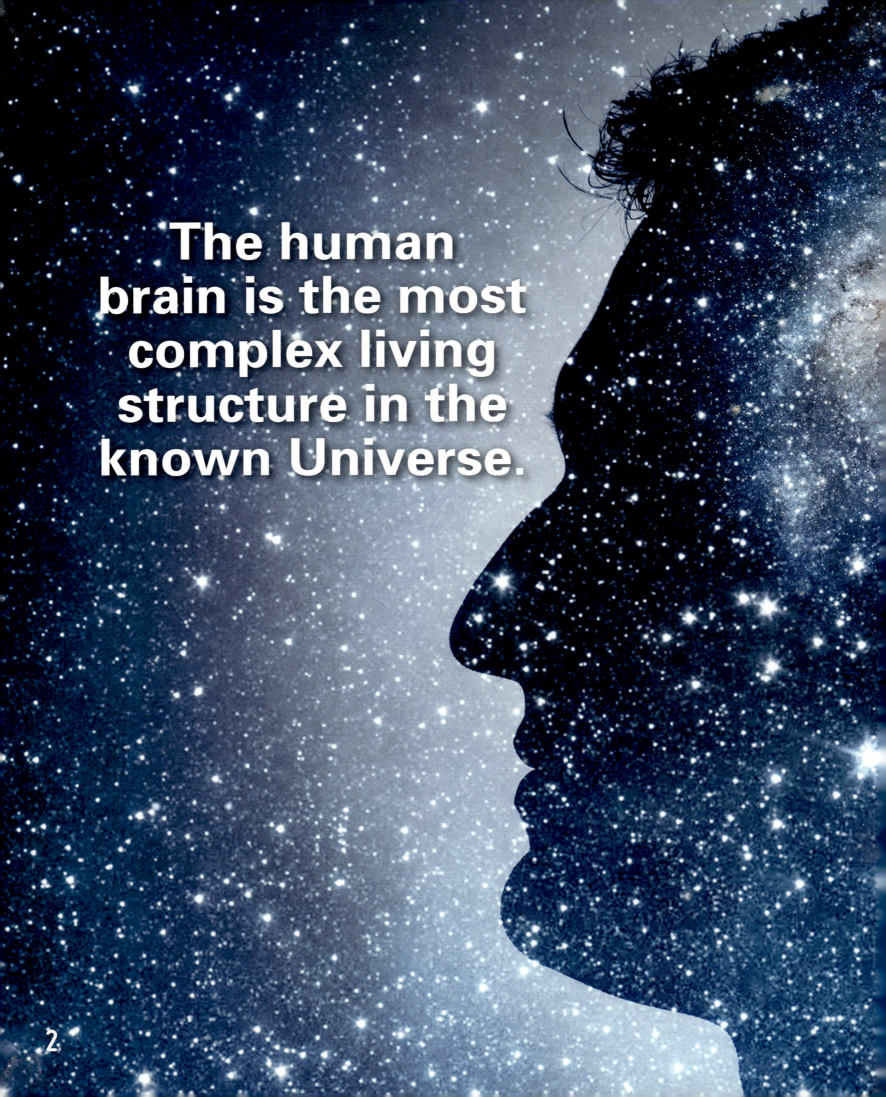

The human brain is the most complex living structure in the known Universe.

The brain is the centre of the nervous system. It collects and acts on information from our senses, and stores the information in our memory. The brain makes life possible.

WHAT IS IT?

Your brain is made of water (80 per cent), fat (12 per cent) and protein (8 per cent). It is as soft as jelly. The hard bones of your skull protect it from damage. Although your brain only accounts for 2 per cent of your body weight, it uses 20 per cent of your body's energy and oxygen.

GREY AND WHITE

Your brain has two types of tissue: 'grey matter' and 'white matter'. White matter is buried deep inside your brain. Its main job is to carry information to different areas of your brain. Grey matter surrounds the white matter and processes the information.

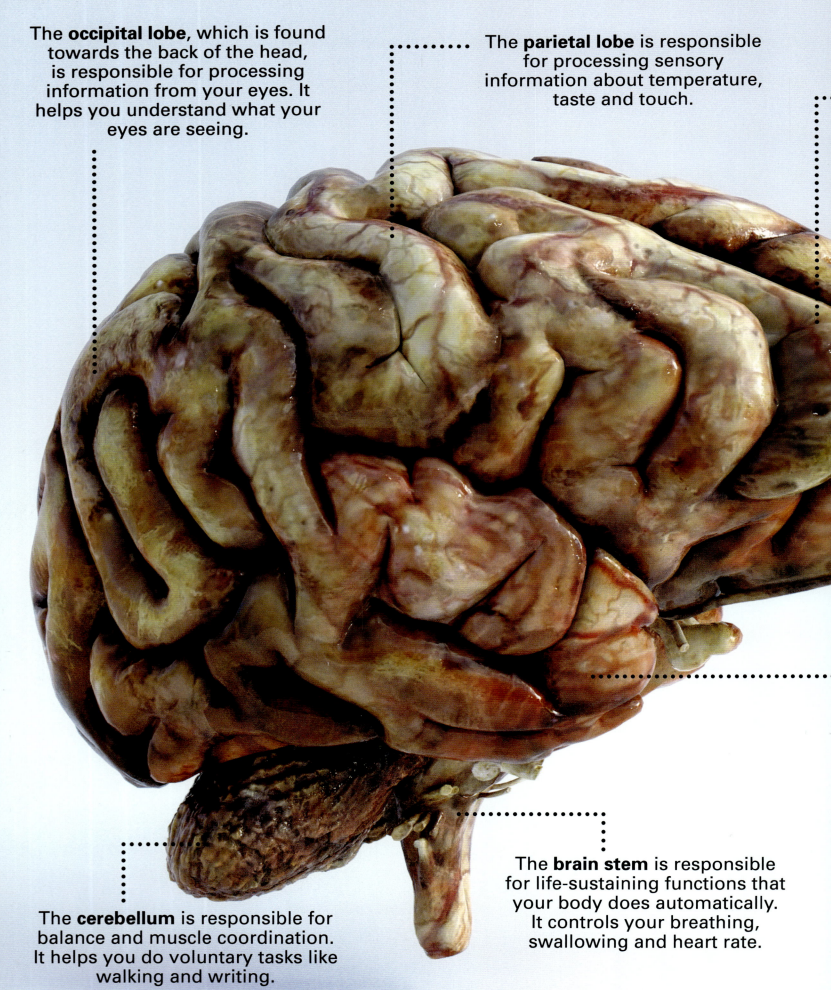

The **occipital lobe**, which is found towards the back of the head, is responsible for processing information from your eyes. It helps you understand what your eyes are seeing.

The **parietal lobe** is responsible for processing sensory information about temperature, taste and touch.

The **cerebellum** is responsible for balance and muscle coordination. It helps you do voluntary tasks like walking and writing.

The **brain stem** is responsible for life-sustaining functions that your body does automatically. It controls your breathing, swallowing and heart rate.

.... The **frontal lobe** is responsible for thinking, decision-making and planning. It is where your personality is formed and also allows you to speak fluently and meaningfully.

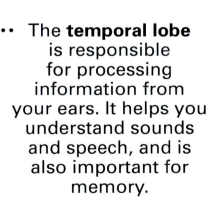

.... The **temporal lobe** is responsible for processing information from your ears. It helps you understand sounds and speech, and is also important for memory.

LEFT & RIGHT

Your brain is divided into two hemispheres. The left brain controls the muscles on the right side of your body. The left brain is also most commonly in charge of language and logic. The right brain controls the muscles on the left side of your body, and manages your ability to recognise faces and pictures, and to understand music.

The **corpus callosum** is a flat bundle of nerves that joins the right and left hemispheres of your brain.

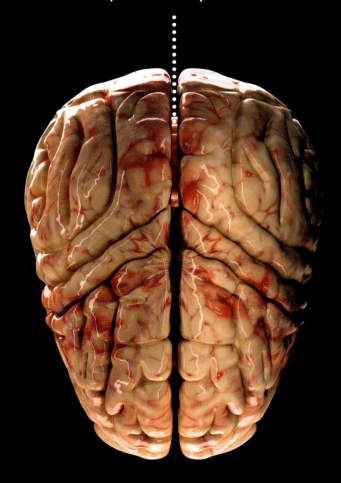

HOW BIG IS YOUR BRAIN?

**Having a big brain does not always mean you are really smart. Big animals need big brains to control their large muscles and to process information from all the extra skin they have.
It is not all about being intelligent.**

My brain weighs about 1400 grams.

WHAT ABOUT US?

The reason that humans are so smart is because they have many more neurons, or nerve cells, than other animals. Your brain has about 100 billion of them.

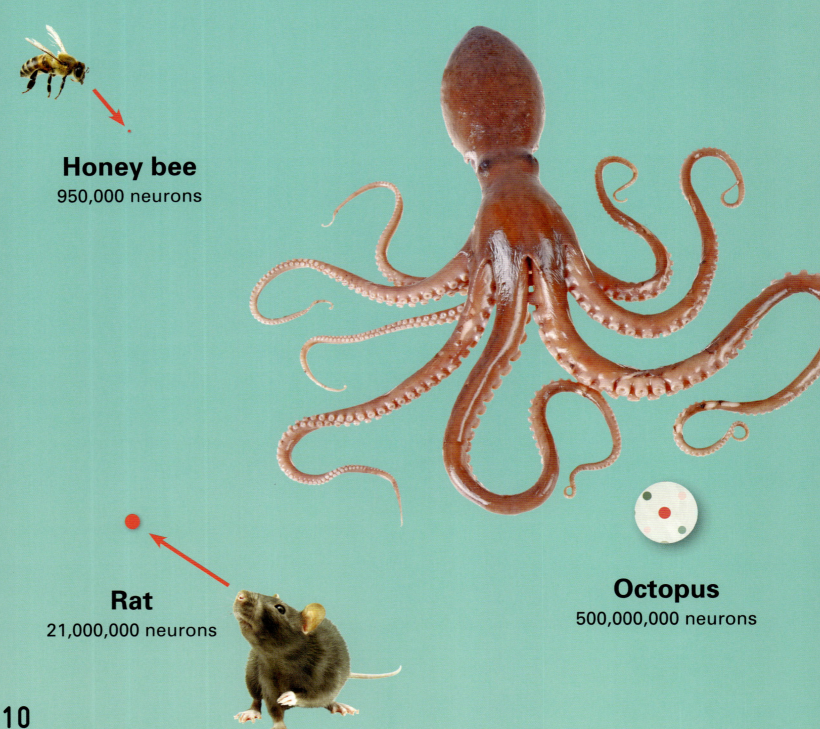

Honey bee
950,000 neurons

Rat
21,000,000 neurons

Octopus
500,000,000 neurons

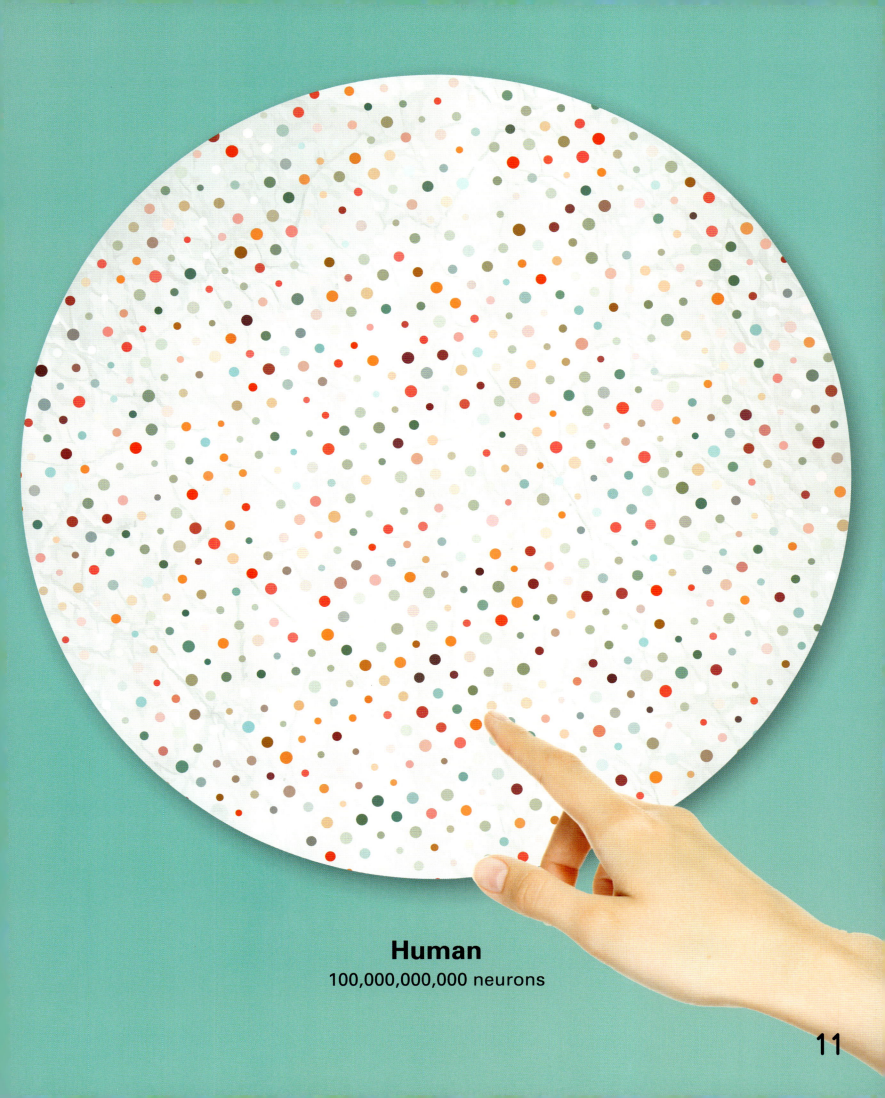

Human
100,000,000,000 neurons

The cortex is the bumpy tissue on the outside of the brain. The more folds there are in the cortex, the more surface area it has and the more neurons it can hold.

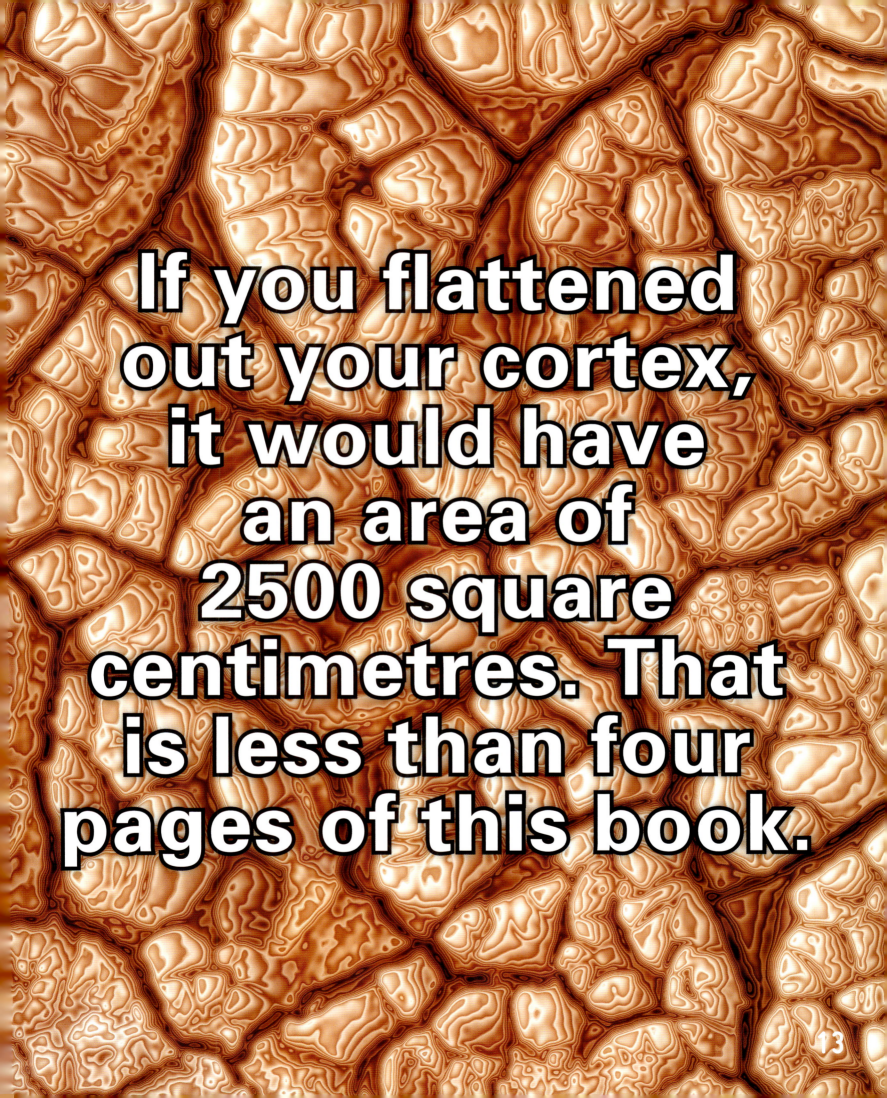

If you flattened out your cortex, it would have an area of 2500 square centimetres. That is less than four pages of this book.

HOW MANY NEURONS?

100 billion = 100,000,000,000

100,000,000,000 seconds is about the same as 3169 years.

Neurons transmit messages using electrically charged chemicals. The messages travel from your sensory organs (your skin, eyes, nose, tongue and ears) and your muscles to your brain and back again.

16

BUT 302 WILL DO

The roundworm is a tiny, transparent animal that is just one millimetre long. It eats bacteria that live in rotting plants, animals and sometimes humans. It only has 302 neurons, but that is enough for it to smell, taste and move towards food. The roundworm also knows to hibernate when food is hard to find.

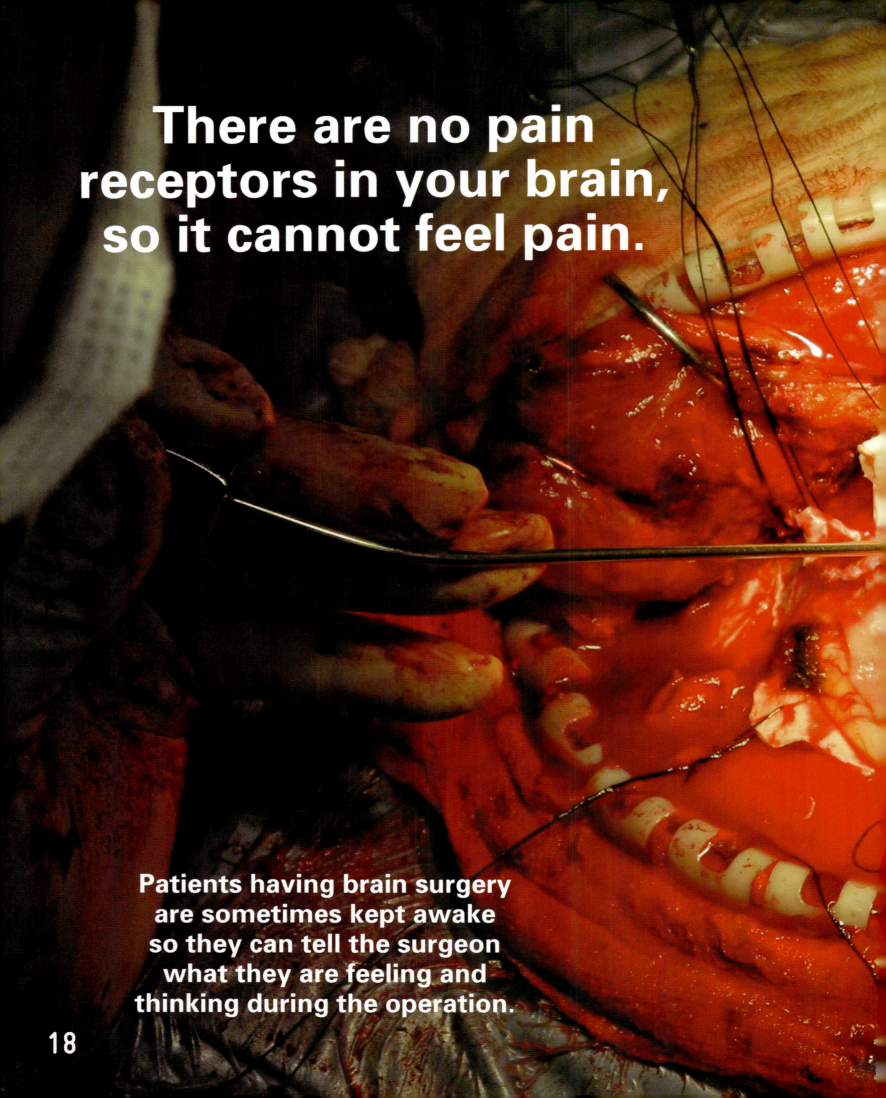

There are no pain receptors in your brain, so it cannot feel pain.

Patients having brain surgery are sometimes kept awake so they can tell the surgeon what they are feeling and thinking during the operation.

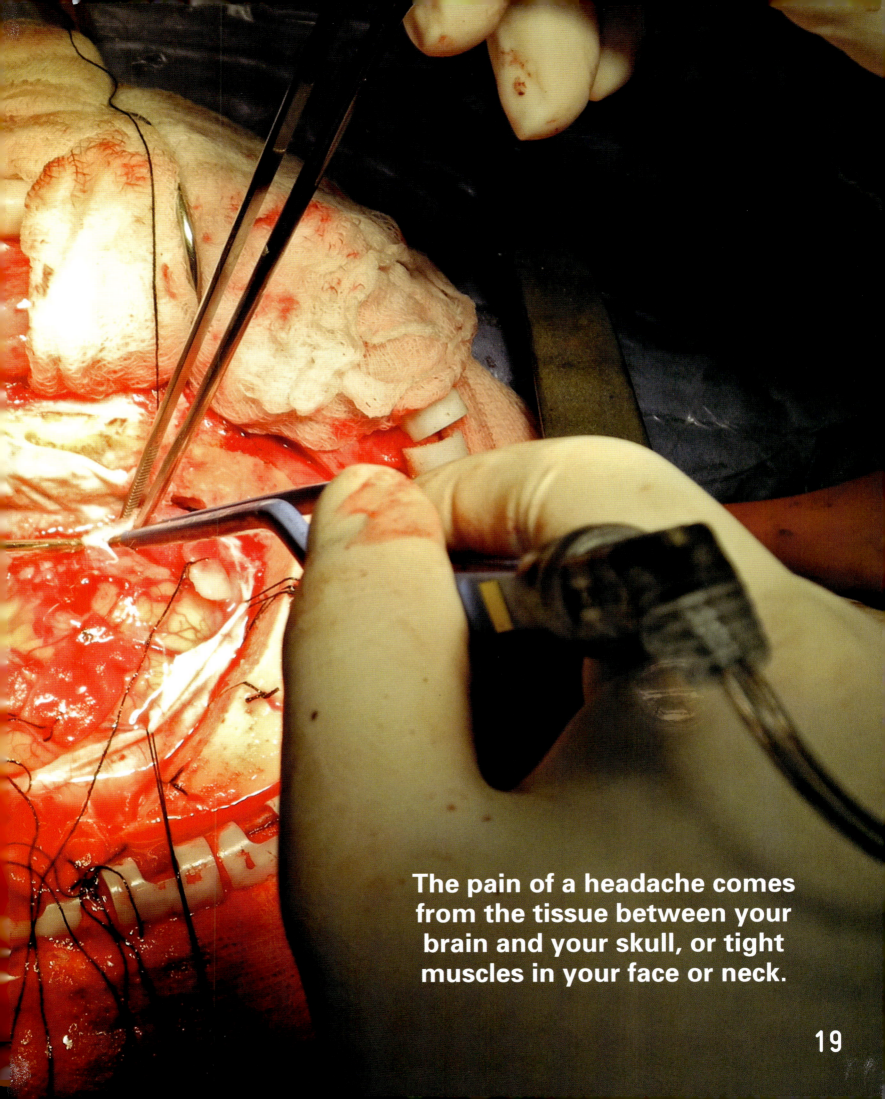

The pain of a headache comes from the tissue between your brain and your skull, or tight muscles in your face or neck.

AIR HEAD

Woodpeckers have small pockets of air in the bones of their skull. The spongy bone works like a layer of foam, protecting their brains when they peck tree trunks to build their nests.

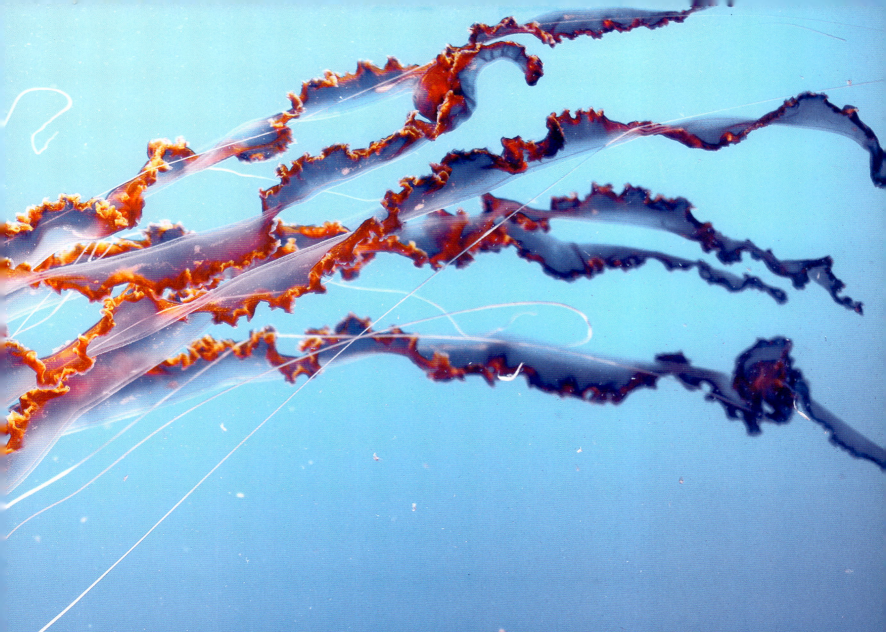

A REAL 'NO-BRAINER'

While the brain is crucial for human life, some animals do not need them. Jellyfish have been around for more than 650 million years, even though they do not have brains. That makes you think, doesn't it?

HOW MANY BRAINS?

The body of a leech is divided into 32 segments. Each segment has its very own brain.

WHAT IS YOUR EARLIEST MEMORY?

There are three types of memory.
Immediate memories are so short-lived that you do not even notice them (like remembering the sound at the start of a word and linking it to the next sound).
Working memories last for about a minute (like remembering the beginning of this sentence).
Long-term memories can last for many years (like your very first day of school).

MAKING MEMORIES

Every time you have a new thought or experience, new connections form between the neurons in your brain. When you remember it later, your brain re-creates the experience by connecting exactly the same neurons as the original experience did.

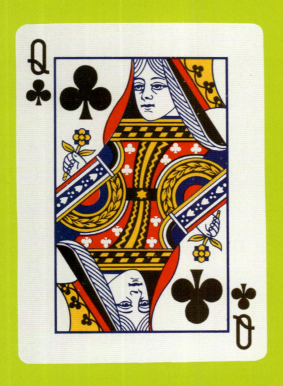

HOW GOOD IS YOUR MEMORY?

Take a minute to look at these ten objects and try to remember them all. Then test yourself when you get to page 58.

FULL OF BRAINS

A spider's brain is the same size no matter how big or small its body is. That is because all spiders have to carry out the same tasks, like weaving webs to catch food. In very small spiders, most of the body, including the legs, is filled with brain cells.

FOOD FOR THOUGHT

The brain of a giant squid is shaped like a donut and forms a ring around its small mouth. This means the squid has to bite its food into tiny pieces. When it swallows, the food must fit through its brain before it can travel down to its stomach.

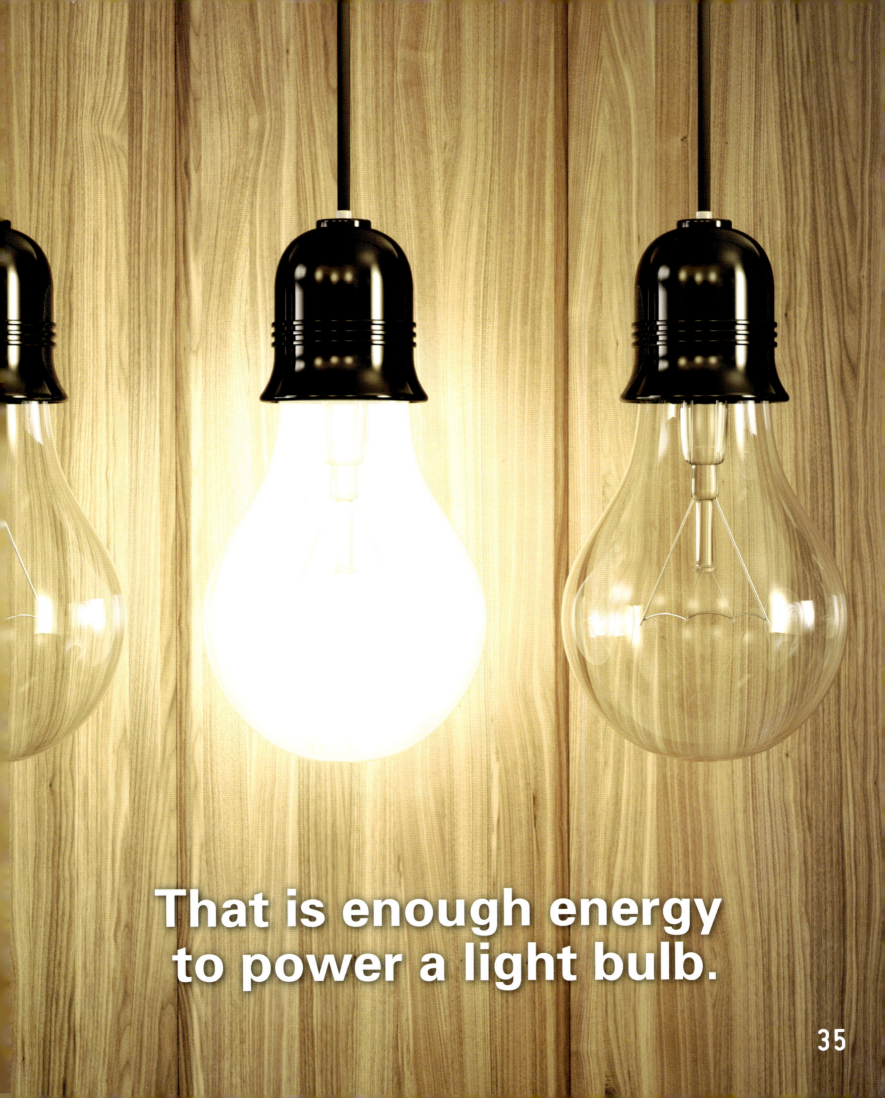

That is enough energy to power a light bulb.

DON'T HOLD YOUR BREATH

Your brain uses 20 per cent of all the oxygen in your body. If your brain goes without oxygen for just a few minutes, your brain cells can be permanently damaged. When you try to hold your breath for too long, carbon dioxide builds up in your body. Your brain reacts to this by sending urgent signals to your diaphragm, which forces you to start breathing again.

(NOT) A SLEEPYHEAD

Your brain is very active while you are asleep. It organises your memories and transfers them into long-term memory. It sorts and interprets the pieces of information it received while you were awake and makes creative connections between them. It also flushes out toxic chemicals. Getting more sleep could make you smarter and healthier.

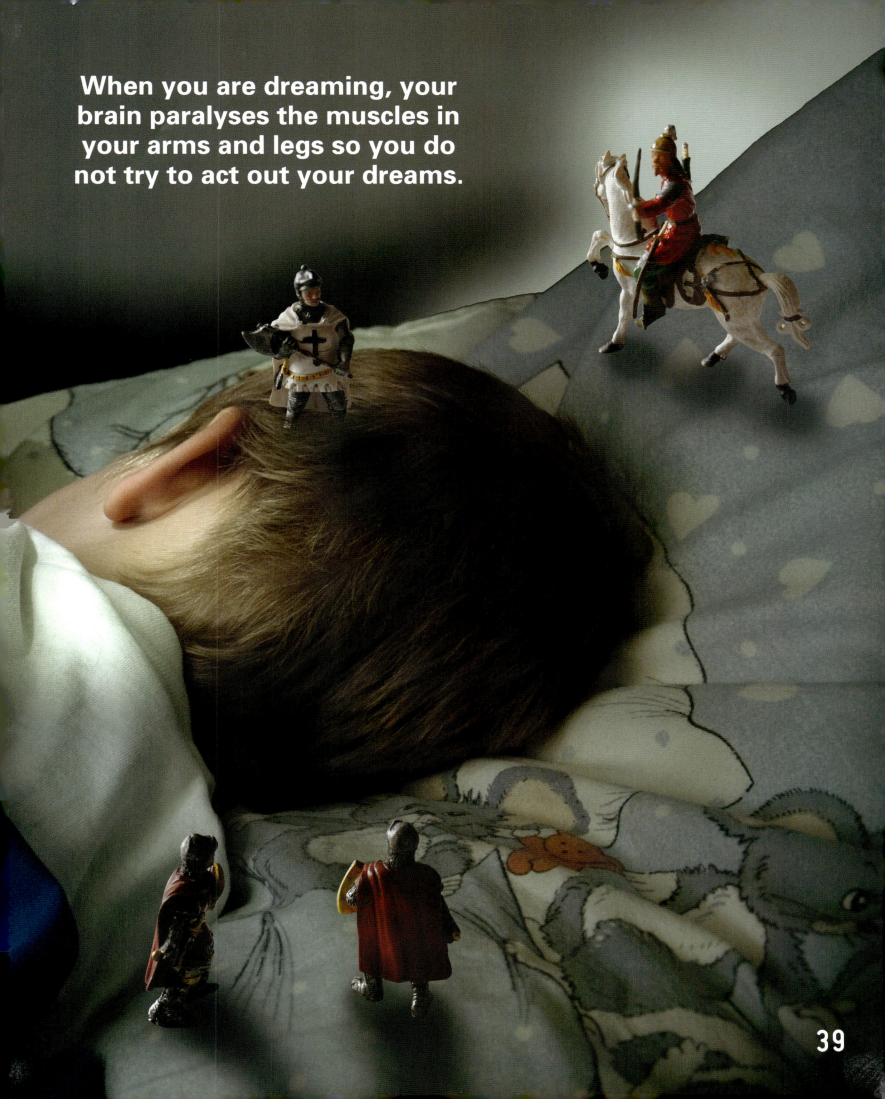

When you are dreaming, your brain paralyses the muscles in your arms and legs so you do not try to act out your dreams.

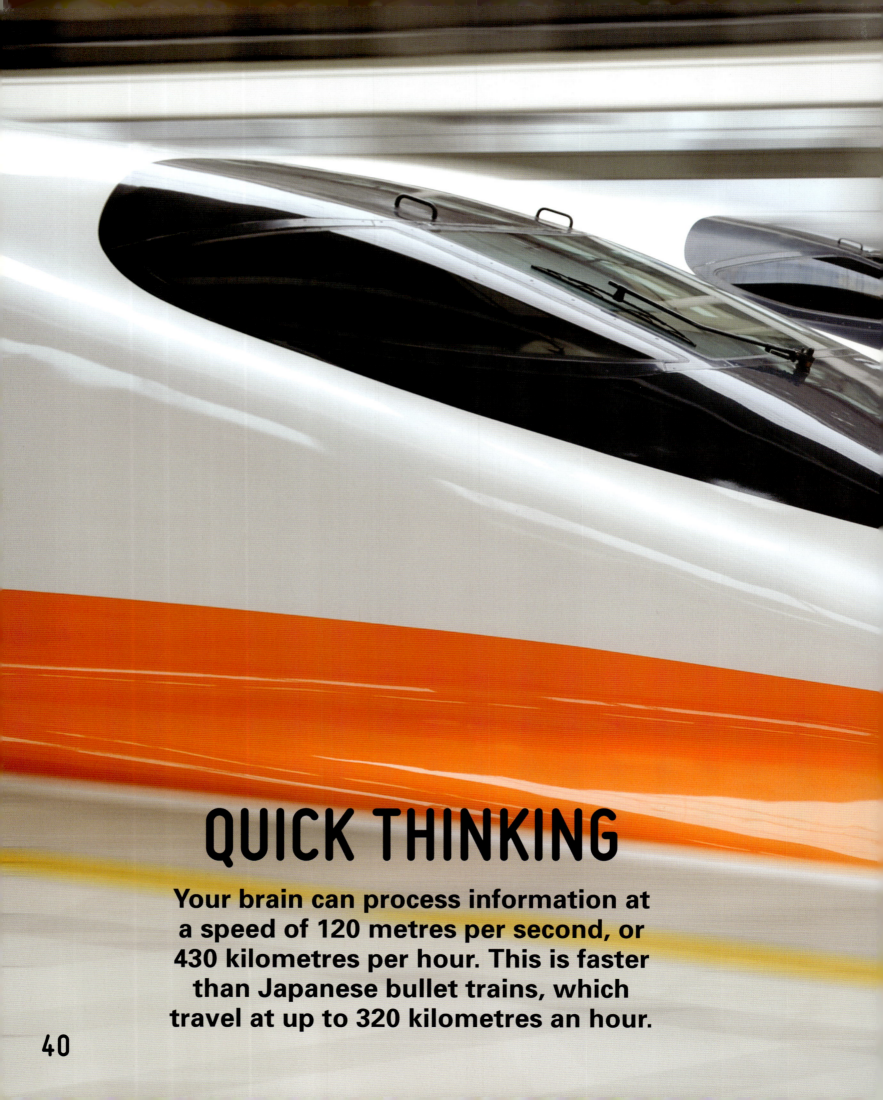

QUICK THINKING

Your brain can process information at a speed of 120 metres per second, or 430 kilometres per hour. This is faster than Japanese bullet trains, which travel at up to 320 kilometres an hour.

LIVING IN THE PAST

It takes 80 milliseconds for information from your eyes to reach your brain and be processed. By the time your brain works out what you are seeing, the moment has already passed.

BIG BRAIN, LITTLE HEAD

Cavalier King Charles Spaniels have been bred for many years to have a shorter nose and a rounder head. Many Cavaliers now have skulls that are too small for their brains, which can be painful.

BRAIN FOOD

A sea squirt starts life with just a very basic brain, a spinal cord, an eye and a tail. When it finds a safe spot, it attaches itself and stays where it is. With no need to swim, it no longer needs a brain. It eats its brain by absorbing it into its own body.

NO BIRD BRAIN

Crows, ravens and magpies are much smarter than most people realise. They have an amazing memory and are able to remember where they buried food after as long as eight months. Some crows drop nuts on a road and wait for a car to run them over and crack the shells open. They also work together, with some birds acting as lookouts while others scavenge for food. These birds even gather in groups when one dies, calling noisily for a while before flying away together. Some scientists believe they are among the cleverest of all animals.

SMART ENOUGH TO BOTTLE

When the famous scientist Albert Einstein died, the doctor who examined his body stole his brain.

48

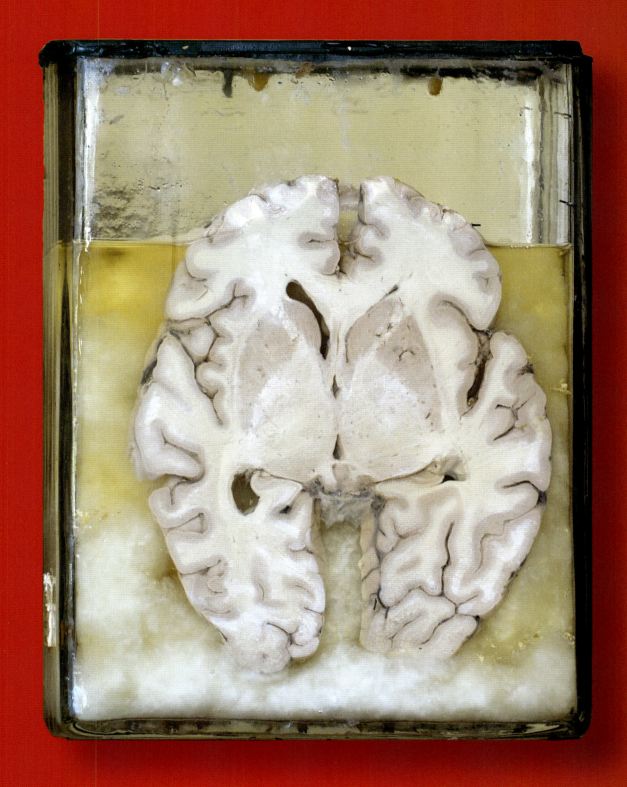

He kept it in a jar for more than 20 years!

A-HA! THAT'S IT!

Where do ideas come from? No-one really knows! But it does involve different parts of your brain working together. Some scientists believe that the best way to solve a problem is to stop thinking about it. While the brain is busy concentrating on other things, your subconscious will solve the problem and come up with a great idea.

THINK BIG
(WHILE YOU STILL CAN)

The 100 billion neurons in your brain are connected to each other by very fine wires called axons. They are so thin that you cannot see them without a powerful microscope. As you get older, your axons shrink. By the time you are 80 years old, you will have lost nearly half of your axons and 1 in 10 of your neurons.

If you lined up all the axons in your brain, they would stretch for 176,000 kilometres. That is long enough to wrap around Earth's equator more than four times.

BRAIN TRICKS

Seeing is only partly about the information your eye collects. Understanding the information is the job of your brain. Even if you have perfect eyesight, your brain can still get confused about the messages it is receiving. When this happens it is known as an optical illusion.

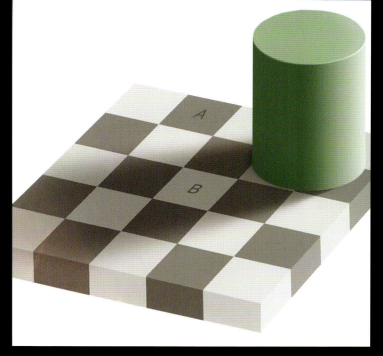

Can you stop this spinning?
All this visual information means that even the tiniest eye movement makes your brain think that the picture must be moving. Try staring hard at one wheel.

Which square is darker?
The 'shadow' of the cylinder tricks your brain into thinking that square A is darker than square B. In reality, they are exactly the same colour.

Sculpture or footprint?
Your brain expects light to shine from above. This picture is lit from below, so the footprint looks raised up. What do you see if you turn this page upside down?

Which man is bigger?
Your brain is so used to seeing parallel lines that it thinks the man on the left is closer and therefore smaller. The men are actually the same size.

COPYCAT

**Scientists recently discovered special brain cells that they called mirror neurons. These cells fire when you see someone perform an action, making you do the same thing. That is why you often yawn when you see someone else yawn or flinch when you see someone get hurt.
Are you yawning yet?**

TEST YOUR MEMORY

How well do you remember these objects from earlier in the book? We have taken two of them away. Do you know which ones are missing?

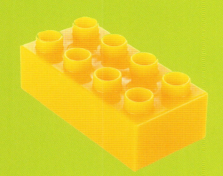
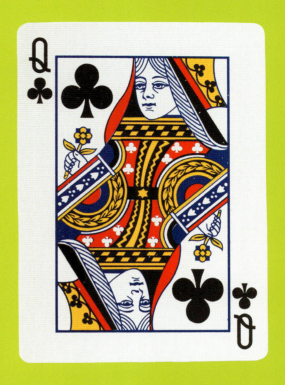

(Can't remember? Go back to pages 30-31 and try again.)

ZOMBIE ANTS

There is a fungus that turns ants into real-life zombies. It attacks the ant's brain, forcing the ant to climb to the top of the nearest plant and then killing the ant. The fungus then sprouts from the dead ant's head, releases its spores and waits for its next victim.

GLOSSARY

AXON — The long, thin part of a neuron that passes information on to other neurons, muscles and glands.

BACTERIA — Tiny, single-celled organisms that live in a specific environment.

CELL — The smallest unit, or building block, of the human body.

CHEMICAL — A substance with a distinct molecular composition.

CYLINDER — A solid shape with parallel sides and round ends.

DIAPHRAGM — A muscle in the body used for breathing.

EQUATOR — The dividing line drawn around the Earth that separates the northern and southern hemispheres.

FLINCH — To make a quick, automatic movement.

FLUENT — Able to communicate easily.

FUNGUS — Tiny organism that feeds on organic matter.

GENERATE — To make.

HEMISPHERE — A half of a sphere.

HIBERNATE — To slow or stop the body from moving so as to conserve energy.

LOGIC — Reasoning based on common sense and good judgement.

NERVOUS SYSTEM — The network of neurons and fibres that pass information between different parts of the body.

GLOSSARY

NEURON — A cell that passes information around the body.

PARALYSE — To make something incapable of movement.

PROTEIN — Something that helps build and replace body tissues, and also helps the brain to function.

RECEPTOR — A cell that reacts to information from the senses.

SCAVENGE — To search for waste items as food.

SEGMENT — Piece, bit.

SENSES — Five ways in which you experience the world: sight, sound, taste, touch and smell.

SHRINK — To become smaller in size.

SPORE — A tiny piece of a living thing that can reproduce on its own.

SUBCONSCIOUS — A part of the mind that influences actions and feelings, though we are not fully aware of it.

TOXIC — Poisonous.

TRANSPARENT — When you can look straight through something and easily see what is behind it.

UNIVERSE — The sum total of all existing matter, both on Earth and in the rest of space.

VOLUNTARY — Done by choice.

WATT — A unit used to measure power.

First published in 2015 by
wild dog
54A Alexandra Parade
Clifton Hill Vic 3068
Australia
+61 3 9419 9406
dog@wdog.com.au
wdog.com.au

Copyright text © Eion Pty Ltd 2015
Copyright layout and design © Eion Pty Ltd 2015

All rights reserved. Apart from any fair dealing for the purpose of study, research, criticism or review, as permitted under the Copyright Act, no part of this book may be reproduced by any process, stored in a retrieval system, or transmitted in any form, without permission of the copyright owner. All enquiries should be made to the publisher at the address above.

Printed and bound in China by Everbest Printing Co. Ltd

National Library of Australia
Cataloguing-in-Publication data:
Creator: Hendry, Lorna, author.
Title: The brainy book / Lorna Hendry.
ISBN: 9781742033778 (pbk)
Target Audience: For primary school age.
Subjects: Brain--Juvenile literature.
 Central nervous system--Juvenile literature.
Dewey Number: 611.81

Wild Dog would like to thank Matt Jarman for his careful fact checking, and Neil Conning for his thorough proofreading.

10 9 8 7 6 5 4 3 2 1   15 16 17 18 19

PHOTO CREDITS:
Images courtesy of Shutterstock and Wikimedia Commons.
Front cover CLIPAREA l Custom media; p 1 VLADGRIN; pp 2-3 Triff; pp 4-5 Triff; p 6 THEJAB; p 7 decade3d - anatomy online; pp 8-9 lineartestpilot; p 10 (bee) irin-k; p 10 (rat) Pakhnyushchy; p 10 (octopus) zhengzaishuru; p 11 (circle) R2D2; p 11 (hand) YuriyZhuravov; pp 12-13 Budimir Jevtic; pp 14-15 Sebastian Kaulitzki; pp 16-17 Heiti Paves; pp 18-19 Alex Yeung; p 20 Sainam51; p 21 YanLev; pp 22-23 saraporn; pp 24-25 Peangdao; pp 26-27 noBorders - Brayden Howie; pp 28-29 Blazej Lyjak; p 29 scyther5; p 30 (card) MyImages – Micha; p 30 (key) Garsya; p 30 (strawberry) topselle;r p 30 (sharpener) artproem; p 30 (coin) Robyn Mackenzie; p 31 (flower) Andrey Eremin; p 31 (dummy) Aksenova Natalya; p 31 (snail) Aleksandar Grozdanovski; p 31 (clip) Gearstd; p 31 (block) Rose Carson; p 32 (big) Robynrg; p 32 (little) Phiseksit; p 33 (donut) 33333; p 33 (squid) de2marco; pp 34-35 vasabii; pp 36-37 CREATISTA; pp 38-39 dedek; pp 40-41 hxdbzxy; pp 42-43 chippix; p 44 Anna Tyurina; p 45 littlesam; pp 46-47 Smit; p 48 (frame) Stocksnapper; p 48 (Einstein) Ferdinand Schmutzer; p 49 Katherine Welles; pp 50-51 EKS; pp 52-53 Denis Tabler; p 53 (string) Picsfive; p 54 Juergen Faelchle; p 55 (spinning) Mark Grenier; p 55 (cylinder) Gustavb; p 55 (footprint) Pefkos; p 55 (man) Darq; pp 56-57 Smolina Marianna; p 58 (key) Garsya; p 58 (snail) Aleksandar Grozdanovski; p 58 (dummy) Aksenova Natalya; p 58 (strawberry) topseller; p 59 (block) Rose Carson; p 59 (card) MyImages – Micha; p 59 (flower) Andrey Eremin; p 59 (sharpener) artproem; pp 60-61 Hyde Peranitti; p 64 Viktoriya; Back cover Sergey Nivens.

Lorna Hendry is a writer, designer and teacher but, long before that, she studied science at university. She loves the challenge of making science fun and easy to understand using simple words and bright, engaging pictures. Lorna has written books on a range of topics, from endangered animals to the five senses, and says, 'My favourites are the ones with the pictures of snot and ear wax.' This is Lorna's eleventh book for Wild Dog.